MATH SAVES THE DAY!
A SONG FOR BUDDING SCIENTISTS

By BLAKE and KATIE HOENA
Illustrated by KELLY CANBY
Music Arranged and Produced by MARK OBLINGER

CANTATA
LEARNING

WWW.CANTATALEARNING.COM

CANTATA LEARNING

Published by Cantata Learning
1710 Roe Crest Drive
North Mankato, MN 56003
www.cantatalearning.com

A note to educators and librarians from the publisher: Cantata Learning has provided the following data to assist in book processing and suggested use of Cantata Learning product.

Publisher's Cataloging-in-Publication Data
Prepared by Librarian Consultant: Ann-Marie Begnaud
Library of Congress Control Number: 2015958163
 Math Saves the Day! : A Song for Budding Scientists
 Series: My First Science Songs : STEM
 By Blake and Katie Hoena
 Illustrated by Kelly Canby
 Summary: In this song, learn how math is used every day, from baking cookies, to going the grocery store, and playing with friends.
 ISBN: 978-1-63290-587-1 (library binding/CD)
 ISBN: 978-1-63290-638-0 (paperback/CD)
Suggested Dewey and Subject Headings:
 Dewey: E 510
 LCSH Subject Headings: Mathematics – Juvenile literature. | Mathematics – Songs and music – Texts. | Mathematics – Juvenile sound recordings.
 Sears Subject Headings: Mathematics. | Number concepts. | School songbooks. | Children's songs. | Jazz music.
 BISAC Subject Headings: JUVENILE NONFICTION / Mathematics / General. | JUVENILE NONFICTION / Music / Songbooks. | JUVENILE NONFICTION / Concepts / Counting & Numbers.

Book design and art direction, Tim Palin Creative
Editorial direction, Flat Sole Studio
Music direction, Elizabeth Draper
Music arranged and produced by Mark Oblinger

Printed in the United States of America in North Mankato, Minnesota.
072016   0335CGF16

ACCESS THE MUSIC!

SCAN CODE WITH MOBILE APP

CANTATALEARNING.COM

Why is math so important to learn? It's because we need and use math every day. Math helps us when we shop, when we cook food, and even when we play with our friends.

To learn about the ways we use math, turn the page and sing along!

When you're biking or with your friends,
you use math as you play.

When you're cooking or out shopping,
it is math that saves the day.

If there's a toy you really want,
break open your piggy bank.

You will know if you can buy it
as you count out all your **change**.

Now your friends are getting hungry,
and you have one treat left to share.

Just **divide** it up among them.
Math will help you do what's fair.

When you're biking or with your friends,
you use math as you play.

When you're cooking or out shopping,
it is math that saves the day.

Do you want to make some cookies?
Get out your **measuring cups**.

Three cups flour, eggs, and sugar,
pour it in and mix it up.

When you want to visit family
who lives far from home,
get a map, and math will help you
see how far you have to go.

Shooting baskets with your good friends,
you **dribble** around the court.
Did you know that math can help you
as you shoot the ball to score?

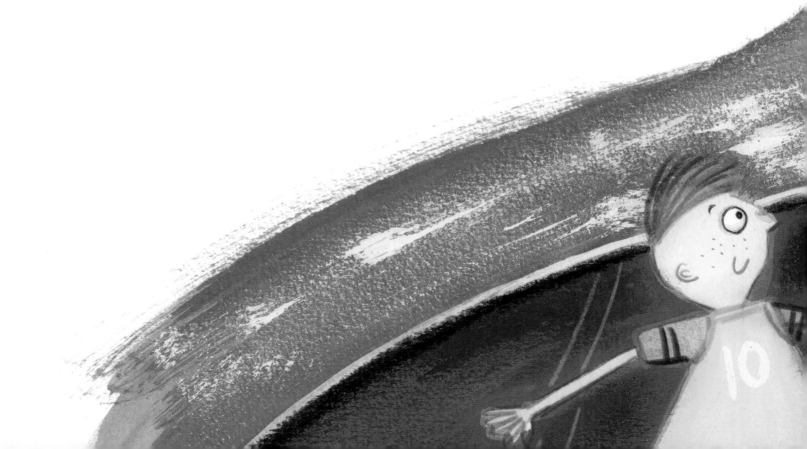

Swish!

19

When you're biking
or with your friends,
you use math as you play.

When you're cooking
or out shopping,
it is math that saves the day.

SONG LYRICS
Math Saves the Day!

When you're biking or with your friends,
you use math as you play.

When you're cooking or out shopping,
it is math that saves the day.

If there's a toy you really want,
break open your piggy bank.

You will know if you can buy it
as you count out all your change.

Now your friends are getting hungry,
and you have one treat left to share.

Just divide it up among them.
Math will help you do what's fair.

When you're biking or with your friends,
you use math as you play.

When you're cooking or out shopping,
it is math that saves the day.

Do you want to make some cookies?
Get out your measuring cups.

Three cups flour, eggs, and sugar,
pour it in and mix it up.

When you want to visit family
who lives far from home,
get a map, and math will help you
see how far you have to go.

Shooting baskets with your good friends,
you dribble around the court.
Did you know that math can help you
as you shoot the ball to score?

Swish!

When you're biking or with your friends,
you use math as you play.

When you're cooking or out shopping,
it is math that saves the day.

Math Saves the Day!

Jazz
Mark Oblinger

Chorus

When you're bik - ing or with your friends, you use math as you play. When you're

cook - ing or out shop - ping, it is math that saves the day. math that saves the day.

Verse

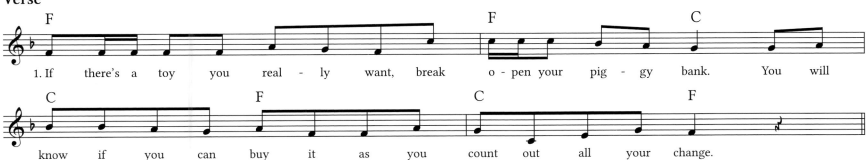

1. If there's a toy you real - ly want, break o - pen your pig - gy bank. You will

know if you can buy it as you count out all your change.

Verse 2
Now your friends are getting hungry,
and you have one treat left to share.
Just divide it up among them.
Math will help you do what's fair.

Chorus

(Instrumental)

Verse 3
Do you want to make some cookies?
Get out your measuring cups.
Three cups flour, eggs, and sugar,
pour it in and mix it up.

Verse 4
When you want to visit family
who lives far from home,
get a map, and math will help you
see how far you have to go.

Verse 5
Shooting baskets with your good friends,
you dribble around the court.
Did you know that math can help you
as you shoot the ball to score?

Swish!

Chorus

GLOSSARY

change—coins used as money

divide—to separate or split something into parts

dribble—to bounce a ball up and down

measuring cups—cups used to measure ingredients for cooking

GUIDED READING ACTIVITIES

1. In this story, kids use math when they go to the grocery store, bake cookies, and play basketball. What are some other daily uses of math?

2. On page 9, a girl is counting out change. How many pennies equal one dollar? How many nickels, dimes, or quarters equal a dollar?

3. Do you have a friend or relative who you like to visit? Do you bike or get a ride to their house? Draw a map to their house.

TO LEARN MORE

Hayes, Amy. *Discovering STEM at the Museum*. New York: PowerKids Press, 2016.

James, Dawn. *Neighborhood Math*. New York: Cavendish Square, 2015.

Keogh, Josie. *A Trip to the Grocery Store*. New York: PowerKids Press, 2013.

Romaine, Claire. *Math with Money*. New York: Gareth Stevens Publishing, 2017.